The Book of Gigi

The Book of Gigi

Volume One
The First 60 Years

Gloria Kim Peeling

Cyclewriterllc Publishers
Lake Forest, California

Ordering Information

Quantity sales: Special discounts are available on quantity purchases by corporations, associations, and others. For details, contact the publisher at the address below.

Publisher's Cataloging-in-Publication data

Peeling, Kim Gigi

The Book of Gigi- Volume One – The First 60 Years

ISBN (Paperback): 979-8-218-48523-8

ISBN (Hardback): 979-8-218-48522-1

www.cyclewriterllc.com

First Published 2024

Cyclewriterllc.com

Lake Forest, CA 92630

Patrick_Greenwood@cyclewriterllc.com

+1 (760) 5192210

Dedication

To my Jenn and Josh

Thank you for inspiring beauty into my life.

Benefactor

Proceeds from this book will benefit the House of Ruth, Maryland.

House Of Ruth Maryland[1] is a non-profit organization that was founded in 1977 by a coalition of women›s organizations, religious groups, service providers, and elected officials to provide a safe haven for victims of domestic violence and their children. It is headquartered in Baltimore, Maryland, United States and has offices throughout the state of Maryland. House of Ruth Maryland leads the fight to end violence against women and their children by confronting the attitudes, behaviors and systems that perpetuate it, and by providing victims with the services necessary to rebuild their lives safely and free of fear.

In Memory

To my beloved sisters, Wendy Peeling and Roseann Hayes.

I'll meet you where our dreams come true.

About the Author

Gloria Kim Peeling grew up in the Washington, DC metropolitan area, the daughter of hardworking immigrants from South Korea. She graduated from the University of Maryland, College Park, and pursued postgraduate studies in Counseling at Liberty University. While raising two wonderful children, Gloria worked in education and coached varsity and club volleyball and cross country.

Now, Gloria spends her time traveling the world, finding inspiration to write everywhere she goes. Her love for the English language was ignited by the tales of Dr. Seuss, with books like The Cat in the Hat and One Fish Two Fish Red Fish Blue Fish serving as her early inspiration. This early exposure to the whimsical yet profound world of words laid the foundation for her lifelong love of poetry.

Her body of work spans over 50 years, with *The Book of Gigi* capturing her first 60 years of life on this earth. Gloria's work continues to inspire and resonate with people from all walks of life, reflecting a blend of her cultural heritage and personal journey.

Foreword

Creating a work of art takes more than merely finding words; it requires a passion connected with the compelling purpose to express the depth of your inner thoughts. In this collection of sixty poems, Gloria reveals more than a series of verses but a kaleidoscope of love, hate, pain, forgiveness, and redemption.

These incredible poems are not intentionally linked. As Gloria keenly notes, life does not follow a linear story. Life is unpredictable and chaotic at times. This wonderful collection demonstrates volatility, urging us to capture every fleeting moment, no matter how seemingly insignificant.

Armed with this sharp perspective, Gloria captures moments that would otherwise be forgotten, their significance shifting between inconsequential and significant.

I hope you find this magnificent collection emotionally impactful and insightful for your life journey, as it has been for me.

Patrick Greenwood

Author: Shores of Okinawa.

Table of Contents

Eve's Redemption

Redemption turns into enmity

Her promise given leads to lunacy

Eve's seed of hope and repair,

Harvesting only offsprings of despair

Mother's wombs remain unrelenting

Her maiden she-guts legacy of knowing

Matronly deliverer names her appointed,

All her hopefuls rise up

But none are the anointed

Great, grand, all lovely bearers of redeemers

Forsake the enemy and petition your deliverer

Dear sisters, dear daughters

Our achievement lies not in our chasm

Our lady openings are but a vacuum

Our triumph rests secretly hidden inward,

Where peace and love are held private

Secretly waiting for our deepest union

Where our innermost private wants,

Connect with our sacred talents

Girls

Beautiful girl

Everybody listen

Ugly girl

Nobody care

Being told

Is same as knowing

Being told and told

Becomes believing

And how girls are told so well

Continually never stopping

Fat girls are good for poking

Skinny ones for craving

Fat girls are good at kicking

Skinny ones for dancing

Fat and ugly girls are smart

They learn so well

Beautiful and skinny ones, too

They were taught well

Knowing and being taught

Is not the same as truth

All girls are divine

Life-giving

A new teaching

That needs speaking

All girls deserve loving

Unseen

Crowded shelters, see them all

Covered in corners

Like horse's stalls

Blinders on the left

Blinders on the right

Opened eyes in the front

No one perceives

It's always night

Stomping

Kicking

Screams of mental duress

No one sees her abyss

Until the blade hits the bed

But even stallions see no red

Bound

Calloused balls of fairy-like tootsies

Bound and wrapped ever so tightly

Fabricated to fashion a foot so dainty

Disguising the agony and all the bruising

Embraced tradition

Toe-curling devotion

Masking her injured limb

Revealing her erotic offering

Geisha

Calloused balls

Fairylike tootsies

Bound, wrapped

Trapped tightly

Silenced cherry lips

For each disfigured limb

Enhanced beauty

Disguised bondage

Eager escorts

Craving satisfaction

An entire geisha

On exhibition

Intense sensual suppression

Staged animated enchantment

Isn't it rewarding

Mutually fulfilling

To be a lady

Hummingbirds

Ticklish whispers fly

Like hummingbird's wings in flight

Suspended restlessly

Hovering in the wind

Searching for feeders

Disguised as donors

Hushed tones

Murmurs of disclosures

Equal to narrow-winged flappers

A day's journey of visitations

Vital as ingested sugars

Preserving secret messages

No disclosures given

Is to ask a hummingbird

To stop its licking

Mother

Sunbathing, pillowed on her sick bed

Adjacent to her sweet head

A vibrant garden

Of vased flowers

Bouquets of roses

Sprays of white and green flora

Rumples and creases above her eyebrows diminish

As she reclines, basking elegantly

Singing and praising her pain away

Her face becomes angelic

Confessing reconciliations

Offering absolutions

Outpouring blessed sentiments to comfort

While the opiates provide no relaxation

Her final season

Rapturous long-awaited moment

Comes swiftly, all at once

With one last breath

Over in a second

She ends and begins

Her blessed eternity

The Plate

Trail of sick parishioners

Guilty, mass crisis of faith

Grappling with dead demons

All cry out, "who forgives"

When the priest is the father

Loves assurance replaced

With the passing of the plate

The greedy purchase made

Tickets to enter heaven's gate

Covered

Too full

Too filled

The atmosphere

Not a millimeter of leftover space

Every square inch taken

With winged beings in a warm embrace

Shouting angelic warriors

Bellowing the master's orders

So loud

So strong

For heaven's citizens

Satan's beasts mimic goodness

Singing songs

Blowing trumpets

Temptations are suggested

But none are heard

Summoned helpers

Providing a protective cover

Slayed by holy faith

The beloved warriors

The cherished on their knees

Pray in a spirit language

Fallen angel's retreat

The battle won

Covered fully

By the Kingdom come

20/20 Vision

I'm not interested in

The same old mucky muck

I want something real

Something cool as fuck

I don't want magical

Fairy dust illusions

I want crystal clear

20/20 vision

I don't want to make

Nice-nice

I want bad ass passion

Crazy noble devotion

Not Tonight

Unseal the widow

Breathe in the heavens

Take no more

not tonight

That man is feral

His bridgework now fangs

Piercing and harsh

not tonight

Walk thru the door

into autonomy

Take no more

not tonight

The fox has the hen

Fists ringed and globular

Crushing again and again

not tonight

The hen flies

Breathes in the heavens

Vacates her hell

Slammed in her cell

No longer imprisoned

No longer battered

not tonight

Earth and Me

Lines in the sky

Write my name

Forwards and backwards

But never the same

The heavens call me

Flashing messages

The stars and moons

Guiding, beckoning

"Be, be my friend"

My eyes sometimes

See the lines

My ears not always

Hearing the calls

Then

My soul opens

From off to on

My spirit unlocks

From fear to air

I, no longer alone

I, no longer deceived

I, find myself in love

Earth and Me

Love's Altar

Salvation sought

morning, noon and night

Not in a full congregation

With a chorus of robed hallelujahs

Or an altar's call

For deliverance

No, it's in my quiet chamber

At the start of every day's creation

Beginning with my lover's call

In my unshared bed

Divine love

More intimate than any man's

The realization of hope

Secured in heaven above

Reconciled tranquility

Adoring love

Chiming Away

Her dreams and hopes of yesterday

Chime-like bells 100 meters away

Hanging on just by the belfry

Battered and weathered by 1000 storms

Unrealized adventures and visions

Clang away a life of no harm

Deafening ringing

The higher they are placed

Unmet goals

Unintended inferior loves

That cookie I just ate

Time to stop the toll

The ringing must stop

Grab a gong

Grab the mallet

Strike, beat, bang

Awaken your dreams

Strap on your artistry

Confess your talents

Accept your uniqueness

Partake in all of them

Play your gong

Abandon the tower

No chimes from afar

Bang it out

From your heart

Shhhhh

Secrets too destructive to tell

Hush-hush murmurs of failures

Too painful to share

Thoughts from deeds long gone

Yet in my soul lingers on and on

Past dead sins buried

Are once, twice…

Born again and again

A sanctuary of despair

Constructed by guilt

Living is breathing

All the while dying

Crying and asking

Am I going to hell

Her Song

Can joy in her broken heart

Be left undead

And grow instead

Can a mute sing a song

A melody in her heart

Of her girly yearnings

Longings never heard

Wanting's never said

Imaginary Friends

All alone little girl

In a box of sand

Are you playing with the friends

Existing only in your head

Are you always first

Is it always your turn

Are you always the winner

Never feeling like a loser

Are you prettier than the others

Always the beauty queen

Now you're grown

Games are over

Imaginary friends

Are no longer

Gone and buried

In a box of sand

Time to heal and mend

Not for approval

100 hurts 1000 losses

For one big win

Self aware, content

Peace within

Last Call

His eyes

Unblurred

Blue green

Stay put

Way beyond me

His one liner

Hits the bar

It's dewy whisper

Meets my neck

Stirring immediately

To my left

No movement

All activity gone

His eyes now translucent

Luminates

Welcomes

Opens

My unused heart

Clearing flight

In my untouched sky

Familiar stratosphere

Too dark for flight

His eyes

Blue green

Remain

Way beyond

Last call

Glory

Our boasting

Self-glory

Disgusting

Claims for what is not our own

Deflecting glory

From the truth

To self-deceit

Planting seeds

Where pride is sown

Our honor of others

Our lips full of praise

To self-achieve

We think of God as if we

Are his greatest claim

True humility

God is glory

Mother Nature is beauty

Be uplifters

Lovers of others

Not glory seekers

Icelandic Dream

The eagle dives

My shoulders shiver

Dancing to glaciers

As my lover whispers

Walls of blue

Melting in tune

I breathe and swim

In an Icelandic Ocean

Heartache

A thousand dreams of tomorrow

Turns into sad sorrows

That cannot be removed in a day

Oh, how I wish they could

They lead me astray

Far away from my brain

My tears falling like rain

My long nails turn to paws

Clawing at the wall

Looking for an escape

Only to find

It's my heart

My soul too

Screaming in pain

Her Crusade

Armored with bravery

Wearing unbecoming open wounds

Covered only in a purple robe

To Avalon her quest continues

The maiden warrior

Journeys with her clandestine companion

To hidden mountains

Where the skies are low

The high places

Where pinks and blues

Arise out of every hue

Now a skillful dancer

To her crusade continues

Parading him to the healing highlands

Her hero's death

His refuge

Shipwrecked

That place of lack

She grew up on

Uncherished and misled

To a wide-open ocean

With no arms to swim

No legs to tread

Adrift

On an abandon ship

With no crewmates

Wild and desperate

Hunting for her captain

Always looking

But never seeing

She crashes that ship

Death to the voyage

New travels ahead

Self-rescued to her new land

Her exodus

To her place of love

Hills with peace

Valleys with grace

Where now she lives instead

Gospel truth revealed

Love and love only

Frees and gives and heals

A captain no longer required

She navigates her own ship

Jezebel

Jezebel, Jezebel

You fallen queen

Please sit down

Stop turning yourself

Inside out

No need to hurt others

It's just your insecurities

A loud laugh

A long sleep

Self love

Divine wisdom

A change of beliefs

Is really all you need

Then you can feast

Sitting in peace

Shattered Free

My arms lift and extend to the sea

Attempting to cross the vast space

Between calm and disgrace

I cry and pray

Please, please

Come home to me

Streaks of love

Line the beach

In shades of dried tears

Illuminated honesty

Amongst the broken shells

My heart shattered answers

With a mystical revelation

You need to emancipate

I am no longer attached to thee

Pleading turned to grief

Grieving turned to power

I say willingly

Goodbye my lover

I now show up for me

Never again begging

For you to come back

For you see

I am home

Alone but free

Rainbow Clouds

Feathered peacock twine

Gathered in clouds up high

Besprinkled multicolored strokes

Shiny but not gawdy

Brilliant

Lovely

Suggesting

Gesturing

The Sacred signing

Magical brushstrokes

Of an unbroken spectrum

Favorable reassurance

The blues are necessary

To have the rosy

Kisses

Lucious kisses

Not traditional

Nor ordinary or routine

Newly created tastebuds

Still classic

But not crisp and flat

Deconstructed pleasure

Textured

Warm and seasoned

Not too salty or sweet

Flavorful and heavy

Like creamy rice congee

Or flavors from Italy

Unfamiliar tastes

Elevating the basic

There's no limit

Don't stay complacent

Moisten those lips

And just keep kissing

The Once Important

Closed my eyes

Recognized lost faces

The cute blond one

At the water fountain

Freckled faced

Laced in his converse

Rehearsed cool strut

Down fifth grade hallway

Sly and flirtatious

My first heart giveaway

The brunette beauty

Assigned to assist

Walked home everyday

From fourth to sixth

Checkers on Friday

Pizzas on Saturdays

Seventh to ninth

First, sip of a fifth

Pom poms afterschool

Summers at the pool

My first lost friend

Three years to the end

I still don't know why

Oh yeah…

That's right

It's that all important

First real boyfriend

Tenth to Twelve

And even a little beyond

Once again…

Why

Numerous young beings

Now old and reinvented

Reflect back

Memories turned into imaginations

Caught between childhood

College, career, and children

Sixty years later

My mind wonders

Ponders on what happened

Now in 2024

I wonder about the once-important

Smiling and hoping

They are all living

Strutting, flirting, assisting, skating, kissing…

Labor

Comfort without struggle

Never rests in success

Treasure chests of the mundane

Always are filled with regret

Winning without labor

Never ends in celebration

Donkey hauling

Tough grinding

Taking the uphill

To reach your mountain

Travailing and toiling

Results not in tribulation

Rather a glorious jubilation

Drudgery and effort

Necessary for happiness

Accomplishment and triumph

Payments

That stillness he bought me

Not the kind in a forbidden forest

With enemies hidden underneath

Or ones lost at sea

Fear of drowning

Dying of thirst

Waiting for salvation

Or Hades

Certainly not on any longlist

For it rarely exists

Trustworthy, free

Unconditional

Complimentary

Except my crow's feet

Lines on our faces

Small, beautiful payments

For a lifetime

Of happiness

More importantly

Perseverance

Nature and Nurture

By nature, she sings

By nurture, she breathes

By nature, she marvels

By nurture, doesn't question

By nature, she creates

By nurture, she breaks

By nature, she twirls

By nurture, she burrows

Straight and narrow

Free and flowing

Nature or nurture

Made or created

Not the same

Birthed or constructed

One, both or neither

Surrendered

Black swirls twirl in front of me

Hypnotizing my chi

Shadows of the trees

Imprint the green carpet

As a gateway for me

No longer in concrete

Grounded bare feet

Rooted with the oak

Swaying to laughter

With the palm leaves

Singing loudly

With the black birds

In the eucalyptus tree

Near the duck's creek

Dancing to the breeze

Flowing downstream

Resting on a rock

Wet with ecstasy

Completely surrendered

Satisfied and free

Just going for a walk

Is anything but routine

Mistakes Not Regrets

How much shame can be felt

Is more enormous than a pound of flesh

Any wrong, no matter how small

Doesn't matter to mother

Missed dance step

Wrong key hit

You're such an embarrassment

Slipped on ice

Ripped my new jeans

Why are you so careless

Bloody Calvin Kleins

What a waste of money

Tears of a loser

Too many times shed

Broken vows made

Children sick in bed

Dreams permanently tucked in

My life's story

Almost at the end

Ripped jeans

To thoughts of heaven

Finally at sixty

Every perfect mistake

Every faultless accident

Husbands and children

Friends and neighbors

Every one of them

I do not regret

Tool

That dude is tall and hairy

Heavy with whiskey and tar

Once a high school football star

Still chasing America's sweetheart

Thoughts of potential glory

Excite his foolish heart

Not aware he's no longer a work of art

Now just another tool at the bar

Looking for a love

Only to land a whore

After Years

Kids are gone

It's just us

High kicks

Low squats

A shake

A wiggle

Endless bending

Just to please

That human off the couch

Lasagna

An old fashion

Lures casted

My taker fed

No catch made

Empty nest

Dirty dishes

And debris

Only leftovers

For me to eat

Ghosts

I take my pen and paper

Close my eyes

Wondering

Praying

Please inspire me

Only to see

The pain inside of me

Lost opportunities

To take him

To the sea

Or her

To karaoke

Now they are gone

And how oh how

I miss her and he

Missing them now

I ask myself

How does it serve me

Unshared moments

Like ghosts behind me

Not really there

Yet haunt me

Funny how permanent

These missed memories

Last as long

If not longer

Then the ones

Actually created

The if onlys

And why nots

Keep close company

With the remember whens

And how about thens

I guess it's how

I keep them close

And still marvel

How much

They loved me

Not Enough

The love I gave

Had no effect

The hate I hid

Gave no grace

The joy I shared

Resulted in a smile

Occasionally

Here and there

The words you spoke

Had no point

Complete nonsense

Not necessary

Your provision

Required too much

With not enough

Received with grief

Always beckoning

For something else

After Good Bye

My hopes for you

Hang over your head

Like a rainbow in the sky

Promising it's all going to be ok

My love through hardships

Commitment to the end

Enduring long after

Our last goodbye

My Love

Thank you for saying goodbye

Complete gratitude for your ghosting

I know you were being valiant

Heroic

It's your nature

Say hello

How you doin'

Charm and humor

A wink and kiss

Pulling me deep within

Lost in pleasure

With all your promises

Now broken

Like the valves in my heart

No longer pulsing with excitement

Every cell waiting for revival

All I scream and yell

Why? Oh why?

Then I realize

It's not me

It's you

You're the one

You belong in hell

I am no longer captive

No longer believe

Your promises

Your deceit

My love

I now give to me

Embracing truth

Making love with peace

Catch and Release

You cast your weapon

Like a fly fisherman

Luring with feathers and colors

Promises of pleasure

Only to be hooked

Addicted to you

No nourishment

No lasting importance

Frivolous and immature

Here today

Gone tomorrow

Swimming endlessly

With no drowning

Please, please, I pray

Remove me from his lake

No more catch and release

I no longer can take

Pinion

I raise my eyes to love the sky

My soul breathes out loud

"How small am I?"

Cloudy, rainy, and beautiful

Romantic and strong

The word is mine

Mother Nature sings

Confirming to me

I am the pinion

Connected to endless possibilities

Witnessing miracles

Daily

Crazy

I am a crazy fan

Not of reality

No real-life meanings

Rather magical stories

Tall, terrific fictions

Of gods and goddesses

Covered in love

All kinds of emotions

Wild, crazy writing

Internally a warrior

Fights, not demons

It's her trained forces

Learned inner voices

Seeds of doubts

Watered with decades of storms

Overgrown immaturity

Out of control

Showing the whole world

How to see myself

Revealing the rains

And every sunshine

The sky is never-ending

The days have no limits

My roaming pen and I

We grow old together

Loving the world

Spreading, splattering ink

Everywhere I go

At the foot of every human

For entertainment, education, and motivation

Until my last goodbye

And thereafter

When I have been

Write Me

The writer and the pen

A full orchestra

A lonely partnership

Searching, creating

Page one

To the end

A saying

A tale

Life lessons

For sale

The author's thoughts

Loves and sins

Some truths

Others half of them

Many or some imaginations

Hurts and pains

Cry out and demand

Do not be dismayed

Write me instead

Life in Laguna

A king enjoys his throne

Choice meats on his table

Vegan and gluten-free sweets

In his glorious castle

Fancy window seats

With a view of the sea

As much as his servants

Appreciate time alone

In their humble huts

That they call home

Eating bread with gluten

A surfer toked on the beach

Arises to the Laguna sunrise

Early in the morning

To breathe and soak in

God's priceless-million-dollar morning

Pinks and tangerines

Scraped across the sky

The bum and his wife

Sharing it with the CEO

Movie star and heiress

From hillside mansions

The sky gloriously shines

Royalty, rich, and shameless

Servant, surfer, and bum

Have this in common

Eat, sleep, surf, glorious affection

Their heart's desires

For complete satisfaction

And some amusement

Most importantly

Living in Laguna

Self Oneness

Laughter kisses her mouth

With warm, clammy air

Humming in her ears

Qi channel acupoints

Open fleshy fantasies

The erotic shaman

Tickling her gut

Escorts to her bottom

Hitting the dorsum

Curling her toes

She braces her privates

Inserting long fingernails

Releasing control

Circulating energy

Her spirit and soul

Creating stimulating

Invisible healing

Oneness with herself

The Cowardly Hero

The boy sits still

Crying loudly

Asking himself

Is this real

With dry tears

And angry eyes

He ponders

The gun upstairs

"Easy payoff"

He says to himself

"For my dumb dumb ways

And lack of skills"

Even in this

He remains a coward, still

Stand up

Loosen that belt

Like a million before

Start all over

He cries and yells

The coward rises

Without further hesitation

Becomes the hero

He did not expect

Saving himself

Another day

Lost but not dead

Balloon

Floating across the air above

In a hot air balloon

Weaved and fashioned for two

Unbelievably romantic

and intimate too

Passionate, open fire

Lifting the lovers

Higher and higher

Higher than the sycamores

And 100-year-old oaks

Where the birds soar

And only eagles know

The lovers find themselves

Embraced in the clouds

Becoming the air

Breezy and hustle-free

Gliding up and up

Pure ecstasy

Washed

Cascades of grace

Saturate and purify

Baptizing souls

Destroyed and old

Pitiful and somber

Like rushing water

Over a dangerous cliff

Each rock is a covered sin

Baptized washed away

Mishaps and mistakes

With powerful cleansing

Life in love is reborn

For a whole new beginning

Born again, born again

Rushing Deep

The lunacy lies deep within

Like water that runs

Under the old, covered bridge

Flows one way always

Rushing downstream

Against enlightenment

Away from Nirvana and peace

To the dark places

Where lies are no longer secrets

And truths are forgotten

Love hostaged and hidden

No longer fully human

Painfully transformed

Into a crude version

I

No longer myself

I cry

No longer able to see

I lie

No longer able to love

I die

No longer dancing

I flee

No longer in prison

I leave

No longer a victim

I dream

No longer without sleep

I beam

No longer ashamed

I see

No longer hidden

I am me

Praise Almighty God

I am free

Head Space

Never stopped knowing

It was the believing

That was so difficult

Headspace calling plays

Too busy with made-up facts

My heart started crying

The joyous thump thumps

That gave me all the feels

Turned into empty space

To house all my fears

Not Me

Murderous fantasies

Not me, we proclaim

As we all look away

Wiping our foggy eyes

Stumbling to our beds

Wishing epic fails

Birthed from jealousies

To friends and neighbors

Sometimes, even to sisters and brothers

Self-serving dreams

Dancing in our heads

Success and riches

New lovers and purses

While wishing pain

On strangers and enemies

Nothing criminal

Nothing serial

Not even a little murderous

We justify and say

They are a celebrity

A politician

A liar

A thief

Please them

Not me

Keep me safe

Choose them instead

Goddess

How to hide in a room

With no doors or windows

A human chameleon

A special talent

Or is it a disorder

To be noticed yet forgotten

To be desired yet unwanted

Queen for moments

But just like Anne Boleyn

With one too many

You lost not just your head

You lost you, everything

You are a goddess

And she is not dead

She thrives and lives within

Whispering and wooing

Your precious soul

Back to life again

Remembering who she is

And has always been

A girl, a woman, a daughter

A mother, a grandmother

A sister, a wife

A neighbor, a friend

Not just for all of these

These seasons come to an end

Embrace love

God's creation

That never ever ends

You're a goddess within

Skate Night

Feathered hair

Looking foxy

Satin jacket

White roller skates

Bee Gees playing

How Deep Is Your Love

Hurry before it's over

It's Couples only

Quickly roll to the gate

Showing an amazing face

Blue powder eyeshadow

Bonnie Belle lip gloss

Love's Baby Soft

Pink all over the place

There he is

With the cool blue comb

Tucked carefully away

Strategically placed

In his back pocket

On the left

Devasting scene

That fox in his jeans

Slow skating with Maureen

No time for tears

Janice points with her finger

Here comes Jerry

So cute and sweet

That rink was really something

Filling the seventies

With lessons and memories

Lots and lots of love stories

All dramatic

All short-lived

To boys and girls

It was life

The most important

To belong

To have fun

It's easy to forget

That girl who skated

Every Saturday

With George, Tom and Frank

Kauai

Dancing with the petals

In Kauai's warm embrace

With yellow hearts and green arms

They sway with me in amazing grace

Long stems waltz in my hands

A wonderful display

In a colorful ballroom

Trimmed in hues

O, this lovely Aloha Day

Their beauty swims

In the sea of my heart

And their scents glide

Across my face

Filling my mind

With Uncensored delight

As I dance with the petals

Of yellows, pinks, and whites

Her sweet perfumes

Lift me high

Teaching me my senses

I breathe them in

With the island earth

And embrace them in my hands

I wonder if they notice me

Amidst their glowing trees

Wanting to dance

While their petals lay on my chest

A single one entwined in my braid

I drift across the island

With the spirits of Kauai

And sing aloha with the birds

Where the rooster's cry

Kauai Kauai

Mahalo my Kauai

Spin of Life

She glances at the window

Wondering who loves her

Trying to sincerely believe

That the children she bore

Remember the care and joy

She gave freely and generously

Only to realize that she herself

Did not love the one who bore her

As well as she wished she did

It took death

The permanent goodbye

For love to be blossomed

Fully grown

For the one who birthed her

Just as the Earth spins

So, do we

Until that day

She no longer does

Journey of the Missus

The lonely missus

Wanders aimlessly

In search of mystery

Excitement and photo ops

Lots of "lols" and thumbs-ups

Through the wasteland

Of boutiques and therapy

Only to find tomorrow's

Garage sales and free bees

Sipping through overpriced lattes

Eating at all the trendy spots

Only to set up appointments

For the next round of shots

No longer exciting

No longer fulfilling

The missus finds herself

Now completely adrift

Reality has become

Shiny plastics and animal skins

Botox shots

Ozempic

At loose ends

Purposeless and directionless

She asks herself

The painful questions

Who am I?

What am I?

Unable to answer

The missus turns down the noise

Embarks on a new passage

To the trees and night sky

Morning birds that sing

Up high where the clouds

Meet the sun

Into the wilderness

She purposes in full

No longer aimless

Into the wild

Safe from reality television

Mass media manipulation

The missus forges a new path

Connecting her heart

Her soul to spirits

That live in nature

From eternity past

There she stands

Away from counters and kiosks

She now breathes alive

With God's creatures

Where she has always belonged

At peace and in love

With Mother Nature

Flora, brush, saplings

God's entire family tree

The missus finds rest

Before her final sleep

This is a woman blest

Now to eternity

Our Love

The palm trees reach high for the sky

As my thoughts extend from afar

The starry night sky hovers over the sleeping leaves

As your love covers the thousands of miles in between

When no rain falls, the palm remains quenched

As I do with the remains of your tender love

That dwells deep in my heart

The strength of the tree's stalk gives life

As your spirit nourishes my soul

The palm tree stands tall and lovely

As our love is secured, sacred, and honored

Pass Me

My eyes look away

From the colors of your embrace

Too blinding for my sensitive soul

Scorching reds mixed with charcoal blacks

Lead me to distress and despair

For all at once and everywhere

On my body and mind

Your colors infuse and permeate

Every corner of my being

So, please

Walk past me

Escape my dreams

Let me be

Do not hug

Or come near me

Specially when I sleep

On The Edge

Lying on the edge

With my lover's memories

Where we once lay together

Among the trees

That touched the sky

Watching a sea of a thousand wings

Fly by

We danced in the spring wind

We heard the leaves sing

Golden brown dry ones

Giving their last goodbyes

As my lover gave me mine

On limbs, sticks, and stems

Praying and waiting for a breeze

To remove them from their home

As I fell to my knees

Another season ends

As my love bleeds

The leaves remind me

Death makes room

For the new

That will bud and bloom

Brittle branches

Reaching to the sun

They, too, will soon balloon

Like my broken heart

Where I will be waiting and ready

Alone in that same special place

With no lover in my way

Where the greens meet the blues

There, I will welcome summer

Where I will dance with the leaves

Among the sycamore trees

And sing

With the flying feathers

On soaring wings

Dining On Poison

Glorifying artificial women

Girls wanting to be a Kardashian

What happened to lovingkindness

Authentic men

Fathers and brothers

Yearning for goodness

For all our children

These seem to have been replaced

For money and gold

Love for riches

Brand new definitions

For life and happiness

Profits stolen

Overstuffed and looted

Robbed from the fallen

Taken by demons

Living as humans

While the rest of us

Search for guidance

Equality and justice

Affordable homes

Proper schooling

Enough nutrition

Health care

A clean environment

Fuck the Kardashians

Fire the politicians

We need humanitarians

Let's start a revolution

Those desperate to save

The human condition

Like the Rastafarian

Ask ourselves

Is this love

Could you be loved

Who needs redemption

And the great Dr King

Proclaiming freedom

For the black, yellow, white, brown

Children

Notes to the Reader

It is my greatest joy and delight to have given birth to these poems. Every individual poem is its own being. They have given me emotional and intellectual satisfaction, that sense of self that nothing else has in my life. It is with humility and my utmost hope that this collection of poems that reflect my first 60 years of life will bring joy, comfort, and inspiration to the reader. I truly believe that writing is meditation. It is what helps me focus and dream; get perspective and new insights. Most importantly, it bears witness to who God is and who I am. We are all a book of the bible. I encourage everyone to write their chapters.

Acknowledgments

I want to express my heartfelt thanks to my publisher, mentor, and friend, Patrick Greenwood, whose support and guidance were instrumental in bringing this project to publication.

I am immensely grateful to my father, Kyong Kun Kim, and my mother, Bo Nam Park Kim, who taught me by example that big dreams can come true with hard work and dedication.

My appreciation:

> To Peter Sung Kim, the King Brother, for his generous support and much needed, loving encouragement.

> To Arash Jahani for his beautiful artistry to make the perfect book cover and flawless formatting.

> To Bryn Weber for her excellent editing assistance and support.

> To my beta reader, Larry Yoke, whose contributions elevated this work.

> To all the special people who have encouraged and uplifted me on this journey;

> Joseph Cole for always working behind the scenes for my success.

> Earlene Shaff for loving my poetry more than anyone else.

> Melissa Davis, my soul sister and forever friend.

> Christina Yalenty, my free spirit, hippy sista.

> Susan Quintero, my kindred spirit.

> Kim Matteis, my guru of the natural world.

> & all the glorious women who continue to inspire me.

Printed in the USA
CPSIA information can be obtained
at www.ICGtesting.com
CBHW030841011124
16733CB00023B/659

9 798218 485238